THIRTY YEARS
OF
CARDINALS CALLING

San Francisco Bay Press
900 Timber Creek Place
Virginia Beach, VA 23464

Visit the publisher's website at www.sanfranciscobaypress.com

978-1-7346024-8-7 (paperback)

For those who have helped create me the past thirty years. If you remember, you know who you are. And for David, Andy and Alex who have filled my past 20+ years with the kind of love and laughter everyone wishes for. Thank you.

Table of Contents

Part I: Writing into the World

Claiming all that passed,
sunset craves the day.
Silly. Nobody
owns poetry.

Backyard

The world
is carnivorous –
poets not so much.
We are grass
on a suburban lawn,
planted like a good idea,
fertilized. Mowed.
"Know your place,"
says the owner.
"Stay low."
Ah, but how green we are.
How green.
As if we will always
be young.

Hashtag Lazarus

On days when
#FacebookIsToxic –
those are the days
to #WritePoetry.
Go ahead.
#Hashtag the hell
out of #inspiration,
#art, and #TheCreative.
Use whatever
#MetaphorWorks.
Breathe #life back into
a dead thing
gone wrong.
#Lazarus didn't rise
because #JesusHealedHim.
He sat up in a stony tomb,
peeled away his gritty bandages,
felt the new, smooth skin of his arms,
stood, pushed away the necropolis
locking him in,
squinted up at the light,
and inhaled.
What if #Jesus was poetry?
What if you were?

Decisions

Somewhere, there's what I *should* be doing,
somewhere between the smudged edges of you and me,
between the places where time and things collect,
and I become a bit overwrought.
I look around this room,
this one room,
and I am breathless –
not because it is beautiful,
not with appreciation,
not with anything more than angst
at all the things that have come in
and never seem to leave.
I see them somehow replicate,
pile themselves on knickknack shelves and end tables,
chests of drawers and desks,
the flat surfaces of life that attract too much, always:
a cracked ceramic candle holder your mother gave us on our
wedding day,
(it wasn't cracked then, but how can we get rid of it,
now that she has passed?)
an old gold soap dish that just needs a dusting,
(then we can put it back in the bathroom)
two tarnished hoop earrings that could use a little polishing,
last week's champagne glasses, stems sticky with vintage wine,
a pretty little journal with a bluebird on the cover,
mating colors muted by a dated coffee ring.
That is just the beginning, and I am starting to sweat.
I feel like a sliver, slid into the thin layer that barely separates
myself
from everything that makes me me,
everything that makes you you,
and everything that surrounds us both.
Cobwebs in the ceiling corner, fan circulating the particles of
decades,
I come to a sordid realization:
I am either a mess or a hoarder.
I am either too old or too sentimental.

I am either the person who can't let go,
or someone who just can't declutter.
I ask you which it is,
and you look at me and shrug,
rubbing the full belly of our snoozing dog beside you.
You go back to the book you were reading,
I turn to the notepad in front of me.
Continue writing poetry.

Art Making

Wednesday,
and I put my work on pause,
find my old art bag,
carry watercolor pencils
to Battlefield Park.
My tie-dye leggings
pick up hitch hikers,
bristles clinging to me,
like I am a spring tree,
and they, new leaves.
And suddenly,
I am six again,
wearing fuchsia,
white sneakers muddy.
Uncaring if my art is good
or I am a good person.
There is only color
as pigment meets paper,
act of outlining
softening the tip,
rounding out
the sharpness of life.
There I sit,
under an ancient maple,
middle of the week,
making art.
Finally, unjudgmental.

Cardinal

Mornings, I want to write deeply,
delve into the beak of the cardinal by my window,
pull his routine song into my poem,
make something more beautiful than myself.

Instead, the day gets swallowed,
sits in a full belly where hours and years swell
into reminders we don't get to do
half of what we want to do,
a quarter of what we need to do,
perhaps none of what we dream to do.

See I have aspirations,
hopes that hitchhike on wings,
land on high branches,
build nests among spring leaves and breezes,
strain to touch the sky's thin edges –
indeed, I'd be able to fly
whenever mood or need arises.
But mostly, I remain grounded.

So for now I borrow a feather,
dip it in red ink and affirmations,
lower that sharp tip
to a page in a mulberry notebook,
quill my words in cursive:
"Still," it says,
"I live."

Joe on Jury

My grandfather's book,
"Joe on Jury,"
memoirs of an America
that welcomed volunteers,
peers signing up for civic duty,
sitting for days on that hard bench,
deliberating. Whether or not
they thought him equal
was not evident:
Italian immigrant,
warehouse worker,
large, hard hands,
soft-hearted folds on a face
that listened, observed, recorded.
The stories he told of the suspects.
Those descriptions of the bailiff.
There was pride in those narrow circles,
script inked onto loose-leaf paper,
lines faded over the years,
pages handcuffed
into a pebbled black binder
I've still got stored
somewhere around here.
Shame, I've never sat on a jury.
The times I've been summoned,
I've been on the stand,
countering a speeding ticket
(20 over in a school zone)
fighting for custody of my kids
(yes, I'm aware of the irony),
not living up
to anyone's expectations.
But oh, the way I write,
like I still had my grandfather's pen.
How I long
to make something lasting.

Cubano

To write poetry,
you must untrain
your brain,
forget the rigidities
of relationships.
Where is the mug
of Cuban coffee
you made me a moment ago?
Here, in the sunlight,
keeping it warm.
I'd like to stay here.
Here.
Sip it.

Artist

I'm reminding you to go back, rewind,
even if only in the folds of your mind.
Go back to the gallery.
Wear your dark glasses and cavalry coat.
Be that thumbprint against the white wall,
austere in the art of your own dress, halls
hailing you just for being yourself –
as if you were light itself.
Return to the paintings that reflected you, retelling
your story by heart. Step lightly into the stairwell.
Hear how the right kind of marble echoes your lightest
steps, speaks of the days when your brightest
thoughts were on brush strokes and hue
and any kind of reframing had to do with you.
Hear how the halls repeat your name.
Listen as they whisper it again,
reminding everyone what it is to be.
You were always meant to be beauty.
We all were.

Part II: Mothering

wiser at sunrise
runaway cardinals
returning home

Now Untitled

For everyone
missing their mother,
I offer you
a memory
of mine:
She hugged
strangers,
invited the lonely
to dinner
in her own home,
fed everyone too much
turkey and ravioli.
Sometimes canned ham, too.
And she always
mailed us Easter baskets,
even when we were grown.
All that cheap chocolate,
wrapped up in too much tape.
I wear mom on my hips,
laugh as loudly as she did,
whisper her name,
cough a little.
What's got me
by the throat?
Pollen.
The dogwood
and pear.
You know how
those spring trees are,
throwing blossoms around.
As if wastefulness
were okay.
As if we all will be.

To My Unborn Child

On your second month
abiding in my body
I wonder what you will think
of your mother, multi-mooded woman
who walks in evening woods,
thinks of you, and offers a view of the arch
over the Hudson River: two tree rows

surrounding straight-skirted water,
curve to calm the still, summer night,
while liquid tracks from teal mallards
trail the flock home. The willow grins,
the bullfrog bellows, and everywhere,
energy reigns. It seems the forest
damns the end of day in feathers.
I hug that cry of sleepless nightbirds.

Fishing Trip

That's a pretty big fish,
you'd say,
laughing at the obscenity,
turtle flailing
        on the line,
poor snapper,
        having lunged
at a hook.
The only thing we could do was
        cut it free,
let the metal
make its own painful
        way out,
the same way
motherhood works.
You can't save your children,
can you?

Eyelash

lashes long as mallard wings
ambiguous feathers
my beautiful child

For Alex

Nobody makes bread anymore,
except for my daughter
who has picked up the practice –
how I don't know,
since she's never seen me knead dough
or watch in wonder
as it rises of its own volition.
There's a miracle in yeast,
bacteria that grows like ideas,
stretching against false boundaries,
reaching out until turning transparent,
only to be pounded back,
yet never giving up.
Isn't it wonderful
how it goes into the oven,
already ready to expand again?
Oh, the resiliency of it all!
I can see it in her face.
Keep making bread, my daughter.
I'm learning from you.

Part III: Discussion Topics

Bearing the burden
of all the right things,
honesty's fragile fingers.

Alien

How strange
I suddenly think of her,
on my couch,
legs crossed,
glasses off,
rubbing her eyes
and saying
she didn't know
what love was,
but she's sure
she's seen a spaceship and God.
And I wanted to ask,
how do you know?
But I didn't interrupt,
didn't give her the chance
to say of course she knows,
she's felt it.
Who wouldn't know
from their deepest place
that something had arrived
from the cosmos's space,
and didn't I pay attention?
I let her ramble,
but I couldn't care less about aliens.
I couldn't care less about God.
That's not what I meant.
Though I suspect
I'm under the thumb
of the mothership.

Discussion Topic

You told me, once,
maybe two decades ago,
in this same space by the window,
coffee in hand, face mocking serious,
 "True love endures beyond the grave."
Except now, I am old enough to ask,
sincerely – what if there is no grave?

Don't look at me funny.
What if there's only
the immortality of now,
striking a pose
like some bathing suit model,
gesturing to you, hips forward,
like you're still young,
and I'm still the jealous type,
and we've yet to have our children?
And so I tell you,

no, I'm not sure
about forever love, my dear,
not sure about it at all.
I'm not sure
the waves would want to bear ours,
nor am I sure
sand would care to cradle it any longer.

Tell me, when was it we last
walked the shoreline,
scrunching our toes around
smooth rock and memory?
Kissed each other's fingers
and watched the sun rise –
or set – it doesn't matter which?
Too long, and even then,
that sip of bitter coffee you just took
took longer, compared

to our years together.
Is that what you wanted
to carry into infinity?

Look a little closer.
See how time holds its breath,
daring that same death to take it?
It knows more than it tells,
having seen the tides change,
having asked from whence the water comes,
having witnessed season beget season,
night beget day, and yet still,
the mad drive to create something to outlast itself,
when really, there was never a need.

Afterlife was always here.
We were always here.
Now, don't we feel silly?

Dupont

Love is all good here,
though why we can't hold hands
tells me something is skewed
with this city or you,
it's hard to decipher which.
Last time I said I cared,
I touched your face
and you smiled,
rich humored and handsome,
waiting to take my tongue
like a cat because you know
you can make me stutter.
I'm not sure what I make you do, though,
other than move your mouth,
nod, sometimes try to look serious
as you talk about the scene here,
the way you enjoy how couples move,
like they know something,
tipping into the streets,
as if every car will stop.
You suck at being pensive.
I just don't think it's in you.
I think you lost some somber ability
the day you grinned away my resolve
never to look at another man,
never to imagine him in the night,
wonder what grazing his fingers might
feel like or think how his kiss could cure
even the dark of its own shadows.
No, what you're good at is laughing.
And I've put my hand in my pocket.

Bail

When in the throws of spring
I remove my top
on the public beach,
will you sail quickly,
back into conventional wind?
More importantly —
will you bail me out?

Refuge

April and cherry blossoms
whisper about the gull
that abandoned his bride.
Bird, take to the sky.
There is no refuge atop the steeple.

Haiku

Around the bend,
cardinals on a street corner.
New Red-Light District.

Inamorato

Once, in front of the house,
cardinal on a wire before dawn.
He, red, the color of danger,
anger, or iniquity, thinks of perhaps
leaving for lower heights, some widowed female
on an old tree branch, both browned by the dull hope
of finding new company late in life. Dim

whispering in the street keeps him grounded, though,
staring until sun drops a hint of daylight.
And there sits his old mate, beak pointed at him
in quiet recognition, clouds switching on
like a change of mind, golden at the edges.

Trust Me

I tell you trust isn't something I lend
like a new book you know damn well
will never be returned. It isn't something
I save on my shelf, waiting to give away.
It's more like a person I don't want to introduce.

You could try to find and kidnap him,
but that's not how trust works. And besides,
there's no way you can catch him:

Trust wears nondescript, gray blazers,
cuts his hair short, shines his shoes,
but not enough to draw attention.
He sits quietly in a cafe, sipping a latte,
looks at a laptop screen, pretending
there's something interesting there.
He does not talk. He is a quiet observer,
an avid eavesdropper, an undercover agent.
Trust doesn't go home to the wife and kids,
nor does he have a lover.
Trust travels alone.

Do I want to shower with you?
Are you kidding me?

Gift Giving

Love is like playing telephone.
You remember, don't you,
connecting two tin cans with a thin wire?
The concept was there, but it's hard
to carry words through thin air
and have them translate correctly.
The metal gets in the way.

If I had money, I'd buy you a phone
for Christmas. Not a cheap one like mine.
Something with all the gadgets you use.
No contract required. If it breaks,
we find a way to fix it ourselves.

But for now, we're stuck with cans.
Please don't cut the cord.

Kitchen

When I remember you,
I want you to remember me,
not as I am now, but how it used to be,
through the narrow opening of time,
back to those days
running fast from the open faucet:
afternoons in the kitchen,
the way you'd wet your finger,
run it around the edge of the crystal bowl
just to hear it sing,
or find the beveled jelly jar,
fill it with the right amount of water,
touch the side with a spoon to make music.
You smiled, saying I was your only fan.
Table and counters were not off limits.
There was even that hour on the floor,
linoleum pressing against my tailbone.
How you looked at me, concerned I was cold.
After, we clinked champagne glasses.
You held yours by the stem, as if it were a flower,
blew on the mouth of the empty bottle,
bringing it to life with your very breath.
Somehow, you forgot to inhale.
I had to remind you to take back what you'd given,
lest you forget yourself, suffocate
as I've done in memory,
as I've done in fantasy,
standing at the sink,
rinsing out tumblers,
believing you might come back.
Yes, that must be love.

Declaration

When in the course
of human events
it becomes necessary
to love and be left,
we want to believe
'tis better to have loved and lost,
but 'tis really better
(I think, when I recall,
the smell of your socks in the hall)
'tis much better to have told you
where to go.

Part IV: Natural Order

This tree, fifty fists clenched,
arthritic as an ancient finger,
pointing towards the sun:
"This is how you get to grow old."

Kayak

Something about water brings me back.
Back to the beach home,
the way we'd gather before clouds could,
fishhooks and minnows at hand,
those little sacrifices nature makes for us
so we might understand life's circle.
And yes, early blackness, August air
wrapped around our bare shoulders
like a damp comforter, warming
but warning us all at once,
that deep encouragement to get moving
before extreme weather took the day.
And yes, the fish we caught we ate, Dad first
peeling off years measured in gills and scales,
Mom frying filets in the same stainless pan
she'd used since we were children.

And then, sometimes, the ocean had a voice,
waterfront a silk sheet, yellow kayak by the dock,
sky hinting at orange, paddles already in the boat.
How could we not venture into its insistence,
explore the hush of days gone by too fast,
remembrances of last night's laughter,
children making a mess of the den?
And somehow in the morning, the call of carp,
plopping in and out of ripples they themselves created,
the first croak of blue heron celebrating itself
like the final, surviving dinosaur.
We pull the kayak into shallow water,
step in, find our balance like a miracle, push off.

It is the moistness that seems to do it,
bring tears as we navigate low tide,
salt pouring into our pores,
the sweat of the nudging wind.
It breaks the barriers between Earth and skin,
while everything – yes everything – whispers,

"This is what you were made for!"
Slowly we dip our oars into the world,
remembering to favor neither right nor left,
part the bay's water in the center.
We move away from enduring shore,
reminding ourselves it will always be there.
We launch again into introspective dawn.
Paddling toward sunrise.

Monday Unhanded

This Monday morning,
pear blossoms
tumbling with the wind,
white cloud grounded,
blue sky clapping
with one hand.
Well done.

Haiku

Faces toward sun,
always the optimists.
Dandelions.

Natural Order

Ribbon of sunrise,
pink throws its own shadow,
winter tree
suddenly spring.

Appalachian Hike

December, and an inexplicable wind had picked up,
morphing chipped leaves into funnel and cloud,
sucking the path skyward, sending scraps of fall into our eyes.
How we rubbed to clear them, tearing up as we walked,
racing sunset back to the parking lot.
You don't want to drive in that kind of dark.
The hills will swallow you whole,
fog lights and high beams and all.
That's how the conversation turned morbid,
you remembering our mother as we hurried,
me remembering every pet that had ever passed,
talk of falling off mountains,
both of us catching ourselves on walking sticks
as we tripped on rocks frequently traveled.
It wasn't like we had hiked for miles.
It wasn't like we'd passed into other states,
overshot some critical split or blaze. No,
there stood stone posts, steel placards,
etchings and arrows to guide us,
making the journey more obvious.
But all that dead foliage rising.
Amazing those things we let blind us.
Amazing we made it back.

By Placid Bay
for my mother-in-law on the morning of her passing

These leaves,
white with winter,
spiky seeds rigid, on edge
by the idle lake sans swimmers,
cement barrier
marked "no trespassing"
protecting a broken-down dam.
Seagulls pay no mind to signs.

On the side of the rough road,
two frozen dandelions, still yellow,
look ridiculously optimistic.
A horn beeps off a hoard of vultures
blocking the street. They retreat,
return, my Australian Shepherd mix,
on a long, long leash,
gleefully chasing them away.

Bury Me Under a Lilac

When I die
burn me,
then bury me
under a lilac bush.
Use your hands
to claw through the topsoil.
Get it under your nails.
Don't worry about your manicure
or the mess
or dogs.
Bury me under a lilac.
Maybe the one in the Sisters' garden,
or my brother-in-law's back yard,
or maybe, if you're sneaky,
that one in the park
on the corner of North and something.
Maybe under your own.
But bury me under a lilac.
Dig the hole deep enough to hold my ashes,
shallow enough to let my spirit breathe,
wide enough for my memories.
You know I don't believe
in leaving things behind.
Keep all of me in one, good place.
Cradle my remains in the palm of your hand,
sift them through your fingers as you drop me into Earth,
feel the softness that is death,
and do not despair.
I'm coming back as a lilac,
and lilacs smell like heaven.

Ant

In all seriousness, I love ants.
Not in the house, per se,
but on a sidewalk
or grass blade,
or how about
a dandelion stem?
Just an ant,
carrying, what?
Ten times its weight?
Eighty times?
Eight hundred times?
Who cares.
Look at the beaded thing,
an ambulatory speck of necklace,
shred of leaf in its arms,
doing its job so perfectly,
in such a small way,
never wondering
if it's making a difference,
or questioning its existence.
It's simply persistence
that gets it through the hours.
In a fit of innate work ethic,
it shows us all up.
Rise, now.
Don't feel for the snooze button.
Swallow coffee if you must,
but let's not wallow in sleep.
Lift your arms above your head.
Put your shirt on.
Be an ant for a day,
or longer if you can wait
out the fatigue of living.
Draw in your sweet second wind.
Resign yourself to be

a carrier of leaves, a mighty worker,
an icon of effort.

Go now.
Make the Earth move.

Part V: Growing Up and Out

Nighttime cherry tree,
impending windstorm.
Pang of letting go.

Speaking of Aging

Age fills in
at the edges,
each experience white,
baby-fine,
as if time
reverses,
carrying with it
the thoughtful murmur
of all that has been learned.
And there,
amidst the cowlicks,
a tranquil tuft of growth.
The whole world hums,
and it, too,
is new.

Waxwork

We create ourselves in layers,
molding those thin moments
between every breath,
each day sticking to our fingers,
forming a second skin.
The waxwork of living.

Downtown Shopping

What a thing it is
to be this shortsighted now,
leaning into the world,
rubbing elbows with strangers,
straining to see the puzzling fuzz
of letters and numbers and meaning,
everything a disturbing storefront of ambiguity,
something like the mind of God.
I wonder at the smaller picture.
I wonder what's become of my eyes.
I wonder why my glasses don't work
and how much longer I'll be able wander
before blindness realizes its own strength.
It's quite metaphorical, isn't it,
the way bright light twists vision?
Darkness is even worse,
ribbons of shadow and bigger questions –
the state of my state,
life's purpose, that curious face
on the man whose arm I touch
while I try to read the price tag.
Was that a flinch I felt?
I'm sorry.
I can't help coming close,
squinting past the air.
It's all so mysterious,
and yet somehow unfair:
you live in this great city,
and I in another, wrapped in dense hope
perhaps they'll find a cure.
That gift over there –
what did you say the cost was?
Maybe it doesn't matter.
Here. Take my money.
I'll buy whatever it is.

Neuropathy

They disguise the symptoms
in terminology:
progressive peripheral
polyneuropathy.
Nerve damage. Worsening.
I get it.

They tell me it's idiopathic.
Origin unknown,
cause nebulous
as childhood memory:
walking to school, bone numbing day,
mom in her old taupe cabbie hat,
mismatched knitted mittens.
I don't know why
she was with me that morning,
but lateness must have made
for a great debater –

I convinced her to cut through
the neighbor's yard,
circumvent their windows'
wide-eyed witnessing,
help me slip past
the threat of the tardy slip.

She did well until, by the miniature
grove, she forgot to duck.
A crabapple tree grabbed her cap,
thick yarn suddenly
snow dusted, while
twiggy fingers dangled security
just beyond her reach.

And me there, laughing
at her frozen horror,
watching while she wondered

how to retrieve her dignity.
In the midst of fear
of being caught, anxiety
over ambiguous consequences
overtook her. Or maybe
it was the cold
that made her shake.

Headwear swinging in the frigid breeze,
what did she think would happen?
Police would pop out of the bushes?
Or was it more concern
she'd get away with it,
become used to convenience
at the expense of propriety?

How old was my mother
when she lost her nerve?
How old was I
when I lost my mom?
When did I stop feeling my feet?
Sorry, doc. What?
No thank you.
I don't need any more meds.

Part VI: The Work We Do

Drizzling into
the day, sweat
of an overworked sky.

Remote Work

In the midst of life's 2021 lessons,
I'm forgetting how to speak.
I think it might be the COVID solitude,
demanding silence and order and discipline,
the daily tidying of a cluttered workspace
I don't want anyone to see.

Or maybe it's approaching winter,
early morning frost telling us all to hush.

Or it could be the intricate lacing
of human beings gone lonely,
so much so, we forget how to understand.

Language breaks apart
into the nearly obsolete,
silent desperation clicking keyboards,
tapping screens, substituting itself
for communication.
Take another sip of too-hot coffee
and answer that nipping email,
but thank God it's not
another video meeting.
It's not that they seem useless.
We just don't want to face the camera,
log in to these other people,
see ourselves avoid their eyes,
have to watch them watch us
while we muddle through
what passes for sharing

It's worse in the office when we do go in,
all of us defaulted to mute.

Tentatively, we take ourselves off,
turning hot and pink, perspiring
in the awkward stutter
of chipped conversation.

Then suddenly, we talk over each other,
streaming words for dear life.
The inappropriateness of it all
piles in the center
of the conference room table,
complaints placed strategically atop gossip,
strange craft practiced in loneliness.

No one knew
how much we'd depend on one another
for such a seemingly simple function,
verbal command of words
having become a luxury.

No one knew
people tangled in frustration
would turn into a lifeline,
knotting themselves at the end
of a thin cord, all of us
strung like glass beads,
feet atop hands and heads,
hoping the braid will hold.

We wonder when someone
will say the wrong thing,
and everyone else will slip. Shatter.

They ask me what I'm thinking.
I answer, "All is well."

Quarantine

Days of quarantine upon us,
I find myself wearing different shoes.
Nothing matches,
not the fear-filled air
with pear blossoms in bloom,
nor sun's heat paired
with coolness of early spring,
nor my footwear.
Cooped up but in the yard,
I stand in pjs, camera in hand,
capturing the world unturning.
these flowers leaving me yearning
for something I used to call normal,
the things that got me out of bed:
sunrise, early commute,
light in my eyes,
tearing up and sneezing.
I'm starting to lose faith,
ask where my God went
when all has turned to silence.
I'm starting to resent my family,
nitpick, hate my dog.
I want to rip up the carpet,
demolish the bathroom tile,
repaint the kitchen,
anything for a change
and why oh why
can't they just put their toys away?
Instead, it's back to the yard.
Back to a twig sanity.
Open the lens.
Breathe. Click.

Q

Sixteen months in,
well, I still work
from my basement,
that deep part
of the home,
submerged in earth,
indelibly cool window
opening itself
to the promise
of midmorning light,
disappointed
by another gray day.
I notice my desk,
cheap finish fading
where dry elbows have
sanded away edges,
tense hands stretched
too often to the keyboard,
now missing
the letter Q.
There's a hole
where the character
once was,
orderliness left
gap toothed, grimacing
between Tab
and W. Odd
I didn't notice
until now.
Maybe I hadn't
needed it?
I guess it's okay.
I must not have used it
(much, anyway),
and with so many words
to come up with,
no one could have
realized it was gone.

I'll just work around
the Q, choose
different diction,
look to the thesaurus
or alternate spelling,
justify omitting it,
because why can't
kuestion or kuarantine
serve as well
as anything else
the pandemic dragged in?
See, if C were missing,
we'd be a bit screwed.
Coronavirus.
Covid.
Vaccine.
How to cash
that stimulus check,
or video conference
on a PC or Mac.
But Q?
No, we can navigate
some letters'
coming loose,
snapping off
from the erosion
of office hours.
We can
lower the shade
if we don't like the weather,
slam the door
when the world gets too loud,
replace the chair
warped with the weight
of our labor,
buff the desktop
scuffed by pen marks.
The Q is the least
of our problems.
Who else
has disappeared?

Work From Home

What I'm learning from the pandemic is stop.
Stop doing what you're doing, from top
to middle to bottom. Stop the redundancy.
Stop the multitasking. Stop the idiocy.
Juggling, super-heroing won't help now.
Overachieving is stupid. See how
it works? Edit that slide again, marking
the places needing changing,
go ahead. No matter how often you click "save,"
it won't happen. No matter how often you have
rewritten, held a shallow breath
reading everything for the hundredth
time, just to make sure they'll understand,
sharp glint of monitor landing
in your eye, thin slice of virtual reality
served as lunch, scant minutes to refill coffee,
then back to your seat, strapping your mind
in with you, as if this were a real ride –

just stop. Turn off the morning news.
Go to the old stereo. Turn on the blues.
Because if anyone knows the trouble you feel
it's the songwriters, musicians, making it real,
telling us what it is to be alive, how every thought
has a place, how every pain has brought
us closer to where we need to be.
Don't be afraid to tune out. Don't fear the off
button. It was made for a reason. It's okay to cough.
It's allergy season. That's all.

Part VII: Statement of the Times

Fear is an ugly book cover.
Crack open the spine.
Read past the first chapter.
Decide if it's fiction.
Or faction.

Aftermath
January 6, 2021
Insurrection at the Capitol

3:37 a.m.
I listen for helicopters,
for some staccato pop,
if not, then something banal
I can count to get back to sleep,
perhaps the seconds between
what the clock says,
what the newsman says,
what my mother would say: "Pray."

3:39 a.m.
Horrible as it sounds,
I'm thankful she did not live
to see all that died this day.
Her anxiety would have multiplied,
packed itself tightly against her chest,
pressed the crucifix closer to her skin.
Would she have added more icons
to that thin silver chain?
I try to count my blessings.

3:42 a.m.
I find myself listening for shouting,
some unusual sound, other
than profound replays of chaos,
democracy gone wrong:
the steel barricade widening,
well-oiled gunmen sliding through police,
the breach of the Capitol walls,
climbing the sides of law and order.
I count up slowly, inhale, cry,
start to ask my mother why.

3:44 a.m.
I divide the seconds,
breaking down statements of what we know:
hot mob, conspiracy spread like incense,
tatted man in horns, no shirt, fur pelt,
Confederate flag claiming the mosaic floor.
Not your average person inciting insurrection.
"A nutty," she'd have called him.
Certainly not someone
counting on sleeping that night.

3:49 a.m.
I ask myself if anxiety is inherited,
if a weighted blanket would help.
Not that it matters when
a whole praying world leans in,
heads tilted, listening as I am,
for the sound of everything ending.
Some are counting on it.

3:52 a.m.
I decide it's time I get up,
calculate how to cope,
ask my mother to find the solution,
don my best jewelry and wristwatch.
Let's set an alarm, shall we?
Do something a little different,
this time, count down until dawn.
Keep eyes out the living room window,
watch sunrise stretch its arms.
Watch for horizon again.

Fall

These dark, autumn mornings,
and yesterday's indifferent rain,
the calendar bothered by subsiding sun,
and some made-up bullshit – daylight savings.
You can't save something that isn't there.
You can't simply rename time,
expecting it to change.
What is this, politics?
Spin it and it's true?
Today is Monday. It's dark at six,
morning and early evening, okay?
Deal with shorter days.
Deal with suffocation of the light.
Deal with the evening news.
It's just a premonition.

Dog Walk

The turtle
has been crushed
by a mower,
life leaving
through cracks
in its shell,
coagulated,
looking like cranberries
and minced meat,
poor thing bobbing
an intact head
trying to see
behind itself,
wondering
what could have gone wrong.
And I am devastated
because I can neither
put it out of its misery,
nor explain what happened.
It's like watching the evening news.
All I can do is say,
"Leave it alone,"
keep walking the dogs
on this familiar trail.

Sleep Study

Too-early morning and anxiety settles in,
creasing the sheets with adrenaline,
introspection on high alert, every thought
filtered through the thick wires of 3 a.m.,
the time, they say, the veil is at its thinnest.

Life and death lose their autonomy here,
converging in each breath while spirits
have their way with the universe.
I've never ever doubted it,
especially now as brainwaves sketch
erratic lines on the monitor,
crackling remembrances of everything I didn't do,
what I'd forgotten to finish, and things planned
that don't make a difference in daylight.
It's like some recently deceased is haunting me.

I consider writing it all in my notebook
(they say it helps you get back to your REM)
and perhaps that will appease the electrodes.
But I'm constricted by the far reach
of ideas gone out of control:
How many others are awake right now,
considering everything gone wrong?
It must be 3:00 somewhere, but on the other side
of the world, maybe they have it worse.
They might not make it til morning.
Insomnia isn't the end all of scourges,
and I am simply a study.

Better to go back to the sleep of unknowing, I say.
You can't cure the world with worry.
Whisper, now, the Serenity Prayer,
count slowly back from 100,

flex your finer muscles. Hold, release,
exhale. Pull the blankets up
under your chin, and remind yourself:
peeling the hours away before dawn,
you'll eventually uncover sunrise.

About the Ending

It's all about the ending,
how the thing turns out,
how it lowers itself to the sidewalk
and sits, permanent as history,
a three-ton Buddha in the middle
of Central Square.

I detest unhappy endings,
even more so, meaningless ones,
so I make up my own.

This hurting creature heals
with help from terrorists-
turned-heroes, that poor village
restored by ironic justice.
Three lost climbers find direction
from the sun, the children's dog
was only in the bushes, and a heart,
reconstructed, pulses
on the once-dead monitor.

You're cured, ma'am.
You can go home now.

ABOUT THE AUTHOR

 Katherine Mercurio Gotthardt, M.Ed. began publishing in the early 1990s, but that was two decades after she had started to write. She credits her mother, who helped her learn to read, with launching her passion for poetry and prose. Now with 10 books to her name, dozens of journal and magazine publications and several prestigious regional and national awards, Katherine continues on her journey of making sense of the world through writing and lifting others along the way: Katherine uses proceeds from book sales to support non-profits and community initiatives that benefit the disadvantaged in the D.C. metro area where she resides. When she is not writing full-time for a living, she can be found volunteering, enjoying quiet time with family and spoiling rescue animals. Learn more about Katherine and her work at www.KatherineGotthardt.com.

Made in the USA
Columbia, SC
07 April 2022